Crackers

by

Lynne Morgan

ℰ
Eloquent Books
New York, New York

Crackers

Copyright © 2007 by Lynne Morgan
All rights reserved

This book may not be reproduced, transmitted or stored in whole or in part by any means, including graphic, electronic or mechanical without the express written consent of the publisher.

ISBN-10: 0-9795935-0-6
ISBN-13: 978-0-9795935-0-5

Eloquent Books

An imprint of Writers Literary & Publishing Services

845 Third Avenue, 6th Floor #6016
New York, NY 10022
(866) 876-4488
www.EloquentBooks.com

Cover design by Mark Bredt
Illustrations: Rapid Publishing

Printed in the United States of America

To Dylan
I hope you
enjoy this book.
Merry Christmas!
Lynne Morgan

Dedications

This book is dedicated in three parts:

1. To my three daughters, Stephanie, Kendall, and Laura who are beautiful on the inside as well as the outside.

2. To my six grandchildren, Zack, Nicky, Madison, Devin, Luke, and Katelyn. This book was created due to their interest in stories about Crackers.

3. To Gray, aka Graham, who has given me his innate wisdom and undying support as I undertook this endeavor. We relived precious moments as we remembered Crackers and his adventures. We wish we could give him just one more scratch behind his ear.

Mark Bredt, you have impressed me from the beginning and continue to do so. Thank you for making this possible.

CONTENTS

Chapter 1 – *Crackers Finds a Home* — Page 1

Chapter 2 – *Crackers at the Seashore* — Page 6

Chapter 3 – *Naughty Puppy* — Page 9

Chapter 4 – *Crackers Meets Baby Stephanie* — Page 13

Chapter 5 – *Crackers Finds a Hiding Place* — Page 17

Chapter 6 – *Crackers Gets Arrested* — Page 23

Chapter 7 – *Crackers Saves Kendall* — Page 31

Chapter 8 – *Laura Gives Crackers a Makeover* — Page 40

Chapter One
Crackers Finds A Home

Crackers was a newborn puppy. He lived in a pet store in Jacksonville, Florida. His mother and father had been sold to nice families, but Crackers was left behind with his brothers and sisters. Slowly, each of his brothers and sisters was sold. Crackers was the only puppy left. No one wanted Crackers because he was covered with fleas. Crackers was sad and lonely.

Then one day, a couple named Lynne and Graham came to the store. They thought Crackers was very cute. They wanted to pet him. The store man opened the cage so they could touch Crackers. Crackers did everything he could to show off in a nice way. He licked Lynne and Graham's hands and got so excited, he even jumped up and licked their faces. Lynne laughed because Crackers' tongue tickled her.

When Graham held Crackers, he saw the fleas buried in Crackers' fur. Graham said, "We can't take this dog home with us. He's covered with fleas."

Lynne was very sad. She was going to have a baby and wanted a puppy for the baby. She said, "Oh, please, Graham. We can put flea spray on the puppy and the fleas will go away. This puppy is so sweet. I just know he is the perfect puppy for us. Please, can we buy him?"

Graham thought and thought. "All right," he said. "But if the flea spray doesn't work, we will have to send him back." Graham took Crackers to the clerk and only had to pay five dollars for him because of the fleas. Crackers was so tiny he fit in the palm of Graham's hand.

Lynne held Crackers in the car while Graham drove to a pet supply store. Crackers liked Lynne and Graham very much and snuggled into Lynne's neck. Lynne had to keep swatting the fleas because they were jumping everywhere. Graham was not happy about the fleas.

When they arrived to the pet supply store, Graham went in and bought the flea spray. Then they drove home. Before they went inside their house, Graham put the flea spray all over Crackers. Crackers did not know what the flea spray was. He was very frightened. He began to yelp. Lynne and Graham talked softly to Crackers and told him that he would be all right. Crackers seemed to understand.

That night, Crackers slept all alone in the kitchen. Lynne put him in a tall box with a cozy blanket. Crackers could not get out, and he was not happy. He wanted to sleep with Lynne and Graham. He did not understand that Lynne and Graham had to make sure the fleas were gone before Crackers could sleep in their bedroom. He yelped and yelped all night. Lynne was beginning to think they would have to take Crackers back to the pet store.

The next morning, Graham went to the kitchen to check on Crackers and the flea situation. Crackers' tail was going so fast when he saw Graham that it sounded like someone was playing a drum.

"What is that noise I hear?" said Lynne. "Is there a parade in town?"

"No," said Graham. "It's just Crackers wagging his tail inside the box. He is so happy to see us."

"How is the flea situation, Graham?" Lynne had her fingers crossed for good luck when she asked that question. She already loved Crackers very much.

"I am happy to tell you that all the fleas have disappeared from Crackers. We will be able to keep him," Graham said.

Crackers had found a home at last. Lynne picked up Crackers. This time when he snuggled into her neck, there were no fleas, just clean, soft fur. Although people think dogs can't smile, Lynne was sure Crackers was smiling from ear to ear.

Chapter Two

Crackers at the Seashore

Crackers loved Lynne and Graham, and Lynne and Graham adored their new puppy. Everyday when Crackers woke up, Graham took him for a walk before he went to work. Graham was an officer in the US Navy. Because of that, they lived near the sea.

Sometimes on weekends, they went to the beach. Graham would throw a stick into the ocean, and Crackers would run into the water and swim to get the stick. Sometimes a big wave swelled up and covered Crackers, and Lynne worried because she lost sight of him.

But Crackers was an excellent swimmer and suddenly appeared again. He shook water from his face and continued after the stick. He went up over one wave and down the other side. He kept going until he arrived to the stick. Then, he held onto the stick with his teeth, turned around, and back he would go. Crackers went up and down the waves until he got back to shore.

Lynne and Graham cheered and clapped, and then Graham would bend down to get the stick from Crackers. Crackers, however, had another plan. He loved to play and tease. Instead of returning the stick to Graham, he ran down the beach with it hoping Graham would chase him. That is just what happened. Graham would run after Crackers and try to catch him. Graham could run very fast, but not as fast as Crackers. As soon as Graham got close to Crackers, he would reach out to grab him.

At that exact moment, Crackers turned and ran in the opposite direction toward Lynne. Graham was left behind, flying in the air for a second or two and then, he landed flat in the sand. At that moment, Crackers dropped the stick near Lynne and ran back to Graham to make sure he was all right. Graham laughed and tried to stand up when, all of a sudden, Crackers jumped on Graham making him fall into the sand again. Crackers then began to lick all the sand off Graham who said, "Yuck." Lynne laughed and laughed. And that is exactly what happened every time Crackers went to the seashore.

Chapter Three
Naughty Puppy

Crackers, Lynne, and Graham lived in an apartment. Everyday when Graham went to work, Lynne played with Crackers. They took walks together and also took naps together. Lynne needed to rest daily because she was going to have a baby.

Crackers saw Lynne folding tiny pajamas and blankets, but he thought they were doll clothes. He did not understand that they were baby clothes, and there would soon be a new addition coming to the family.

One night when it was time to go to sleep, Crackers, Lynne, and Graham climbed into bed as usual. This night, however, was a little different. Lynne happened to roll over and accidentally pushed Crackers out of bed!

Crackers fell to the floor with a plop, shook himself awake, and realized what had happened. Crackers jumped back into bed again, but this time, he jumped up next to Graham. Just as Crackers was beginning to fall asleep, dreaming of doggie biscuits, Graham rolled over. Once again, plop, Crackers fell out of bed!

"Hmmm," thought Crackers. "Did the bed shrink?" Then he remembered that Lynne seemed to have gained some weight lately and took up much more room in bed. "Well," thought Crackers. "I will just snuggle up to these doll clothes on this rocking chair and have a good night's rest."

The next morning, Lynne did not seem happy to see Crackers lying on the baby clothes. "Oh," she cried. "Now I will have to wash all the baby clothes again." Crackers didn't understand. He did not know what all the fuss was about a few dog hairs on doll clothes.

Later that day, Graham came home early and took Lynne away with a suitcase. "That's strange," thought Crackers. "Why does she need a suitcase?"

Crackers waited and waited, but Lynne and Graham did not come home. To make matters worse, he had to go to the bathroom. Crackers had excellent manners and knew he could not go to the bathroom in the house. He did not know how to use the toilet. He had to wait until Lynne or Graham came home to take him for a walk.

Then, Crackers did a very bad thing. He couldn't help it! He was so frustrated that he started gnawing on the couch! He chewed and chewed. He knew it was not the right thing to do, but it was all he could think of to take his mind off his bathroom problem. After he finished chewing one corner, he went to the other, and then to the other. Soon, all four corners of the couch were ruined. Then Graham came back home and saw what Crackers had done!

Chapter Four

Crackers Meets Baby Stephanie

When Graham walked into the apartment and looked at the torn apart couch, he was astonished. "Crackers, what have you done?" he shouted.

Crackers tried to hide under the couch, but he couldn't fit very well. His back legs and tail stuck out. Because he couldn't see Graham, he thought Graham couldn't see him.

"Come out of there, Crackers," said Graham very sternly. "You have never done anything like this before."

Crackers peeked out at Graham but didn't feel quite ready to get completely out from under the couch he had ruined. Worse yet, he still had to go to the bathroom really bad. "Moan, groan,"

Crackers said with his nose between his paws and his eyes looking up at Graham.

"I just don't understand," said Graham. Then Graham realized what had happened. Crackers had never been left alone all day. He didn't understand what had happened to Lynne. She was his playmate all day long. Crackers didn't know that Lynne had gone to the hospital to have their baby.

"That explains it," thought Graham. Then he had another thought. "Oh, my goodness. Crackers probably has to go to the bathroom."

Graham got Crackers' leash and opened the door. Crackers came bounding from under the couch with his tail wagging so hard it almost knocked over a lamp. Graham attached the leash to Crackers' collar, and off the two of them went to take a nice walk.

While they were walking, Graham told Crackers how Lynne had given birth to a beautiful baby daughter named Stephanie. She would be coming home in a couple of days. Crackers didn't really understand what Graham was saying, but Graham was so happy that Crackers knew everything would be all right. He didn't want to think about the ruined couch.

During the next few days, Graham spent his time taking Crackers on walks, going to work, and visiting Lynne and baby Stephanie at the hospital. He made sure Crackers had plenty of walks, and Crackers made sure to be on his best behavior when he was left alone in the apartment. Finally, it was time for Graham to bring Lynne and baby Stephanie home from the hospital.

Graham drove the car to the apartment and told Lynne to wait in the car with baby Stephanie. Graham ran up the steps and let Crackers out of the apartment. When Crackers saw Lynne in the car, he ran so fast his feet got tangled up, and he fell over. He picked himself up and continued running until he got to Lynne.

"Oh, how I missed you, you silly puppy," laughed Lynne as she scratched Crackers behind his ears.

Crackers was so happy to see Lynne, he jumped on her and licked her face so many times she could hardly breathe. Then Crackers heard a strange sound coming from a pink blanket. He poked his nose inside the blanket and came face to face with baby Stephanie.

Chapter Five

Crackers Finds A Hiding Place

As soon as Crackers saw baby Stephanie, his eyes got so big they almost popped out of his head. He had never seen a newborn baby before. Crackers was afraid. He backed up very slowly just as baby Stephanie let out a cry. Crackers was so frightened, he backed up faster but forgot to look where he was going. He fell upside down, out of the car.

"Oh, Crackers. Come here," said Graham. "This is our baby. She won't hurt you. In fact, I think the two of you will become great friends and grow up together. Come inside the house where you can have a better look at baby Stephanie."

Lynne, Graham, baby Stephanie, and Crackers went inside the house. Lynne laid baby Stephanie on a blanket on the floor. Crackers was very curious. He crept closer and closer until he got close enough to sniff baby Stephanie. Crackers liked her scent and began licking her toes. Just then, baby Stephanie kicked her foot and hit Crackers in the nose. Crackers ran, yelping, into the kitchen to hide.

"Come out, Crackers," said Lynne, laughing. "Baby Stephanie didn't mean to hit your nose."

Crackers appeared again and watched while Lynne and Graham took baby Stephanie into her room. There, in the corner of the room, was a beautiful bassinette. It had been Graham's when he was a baby. It was white wicker and had a beautiful white skirt that went all around the bassinette. The bassinette skirt was long enough to touch the floor. Graham's grandmother made it, and that made it all the more special. It was time for baby Stephanie to take her nap.

Crackers watched as Lynne and Graham put baby Stephanie in the bassinette and then went to their room to take a nap. He did not want to leave baby Stephanie. Crackers decided he would sleep under the bassinette where he could be close to baby Stephanie and protect her while she slept. Crackers laid down and inched his way under the bassinette trying very carefully not to bump it.

Every once in a while his head would hit the bottom of the bassinette, and baby Stephanie would give a little coo. It was as if she understood what Crackers was doing. She felt very happy.

Everyone slept peacefully until there was a knock at the door. Graham awoke from his nap and answered the door. It was Mrs. Goddard, a neighbor from down the street. She had a gift for baby Stephanie in her hand.

"Hello," she said smiling. "Congratulations on the birth of your daughter. I brought a gift for her."

"How thoughtful of you, Mrs. Goddard," said Graham. "Lynne, come and say hello to Mrs. Goddard. She brought something for baby Stephanie."

Lynne came into the room and gave Mrs. Goddard a hug. "Thank you so much," said Lynne. "Would you like to see our baby?"

"Oh, yes. I just love babies," said Mrs. Goddard. Lynne and Graham led Mrs. Goddard to baby Stephanie's room. "What a beautiful bassinette," said Mrs. Goddard as she approached the bassinette and baby Stephanie. She could not see Crackers who was hiding under the skirt of the bassinette.

Suddenly, Crackers let out a growl. It was a warning growl. Crackers was telling Mrs. Goddard not to get any closer to baby Stephanie.

"Oh, my," said Mrs. Goddard. "Your baby sounds very strange." Mrs. Goddard started to take another step closer to the bassinette when Crackers growled again. This time it was a louder and more serious growl.

"Oh, my," said Mrs. Goddard. "I don't think your baby likes me very much. I will be leaving now." Mrs. Goddard walked as fast as she could to the front door and went home.

Lynne and Graham were very puzzled. Then, suddenly, Graham understood. He called Crackers. Nothing happened. He called him again. This time a black nose appeared from under the beautiful white skirt.

"So it was you, silly puppy. You were trying to protect baby Stephanie, weren't you? Thank goodness our baby doesn't growl," said Lynne giggling.

Crackers was relieved to hear Lynne laugh. Everything was all right. He tucked his nose back under the bassinette skirt and, once again, became invisible. He had found the perfect hiding place to protect baby Stephanie.

Chapter Six

Crackers Gets Arrested

Lynne and Graham had two more daughters after the birth of baby Stephanie. Their names were Kendall and Laura. Baby Kendall was born two years after baby Stephanie, and baby Laura was born the year after baby Kendall.

Crackers hid under the bassinette when it held baby Kendall and when it held baby Laura, just as he had done for baby Stephanie. He also growled every time anyone outside the family approached the bassinette. Many people thought Lynne and Graham had very strange babies because they thought the babies were the ones growling!

Crackers had never been happier in his life. He loved spending the day with Lynne and the babies while Graham was at work. Crackers loved taking walks with Lynne and the babies. He loved licking baby food from their faces. He thought he was being a big help and didn't understand why Lynne would say, "Crackers, please don't do that." After Crackers heard Lynne's comment, he only did it when she wasn't looking!

The days and years past, and soon the babies grew up and became little girls. One day, Stephanie, Kendall, and Laura were all old enough to go to school together. Every morning before school, Lynne packed their lunches in little brown bags. Crackers would try to poke his nose in the bags to see what smelled so good, but someone always said, "Crackers, please don't do that."

Everyday, Stephanie, Kendall, and Laura walked over the hill to the little elementary school. Everyday, Crackers would watch them through the living room window until he couldn't see them anymore. He was very sad.

Later in the day, Crackers could hear them playing outside at recess time, but he couldn't play with them. Then he had an idea.

Crackers went to the door, put his paw on it, and whined. This was his way of saying that he wanted to go out. Lynne opened the door for Crackers, and out he went. In those days there was no leash law, and dogs could roam as they pleased.

Crackers headed straight for the little elementary school where he knew he would find Stephanie, Kendall, and Laura. In fact, he could hear them playing outside because it was recess time. As he ran over the hill to the school, he suddenly stopped in his tracks. There, right in front of him, were about five little brown lunch bags. Some of the children had brought their lunches with them because they would be going to the cafeteria directly after recess.

Crackers could not believe his luck. He forgot completely about visiting Stephanie, Kendall, and Laura and went straight for the lunch bags. He picked up one and shook it until a yummy peanut butter sandwich fell out. Crackers gobbled up the peanut butter sandwich. He shook another bag, and out came a ham and cheese sandwich. Crackers gobbled that up too. He was having a wonderful time until a little boy saw Crackers eating his sandwich and ran crying to his teacher.

Soon after, the bell rang. Everyone had to go inside, and the children had to leave their lunches behind. The teacher was afraid that Crackers was a mean dog, and she did not want the children to go near him. In fact, she called the police to come and take Crackers away.

Stephanie, Kendall, and Laura knew the thief was Crackers because they had seen him eating the sandwiches when everyone was yelling and pointing at him. They were too embarrassed to tell anyone that Crackers was their dog. They did not know a policeman was called to take Crackers away.

Fortunately, when the policeman approached Crackers, he could tell that Crackers was a friendly dog. Crackers was happy to see the policeman and thought he might like to play.

"Hello, doggie," said the policeman.

Crackers jumped up and wagged his tail.

"Let me see your collar, doggie," said the policeman.

Crackers stood still as the policeman examined his collar. On the collar was a tag that listed his name and address. The policeman decided to give Crackers another chance.

The policeman picked up Crackers and put him in the back of his truck, which was surrounded by a net. Therefore, Crackers could not jump out.

"Hmmm," thought Crackers. "This does not seem right. I think I'm in trouble."

Then the policeman drove Crackers home. Lynne was looking out the window just as the policeman's truck pulled into the driveway. "What on earth is this all about?" she thought. She opened the door as the policeman was coming up the front walk. At the same time, she saw a very ashamed Crackers peering out at her through the netting in the back of the truck.

"Is this your dog, ma'm?" asked the policeman.

"Yes, he is," answered Lynne. "What did he do?"

"He has been stealing lunch bags from the children at Kennedy School," responded the policeman.

"Oh," said Lynne. "I am so sorry. He is really a good dog, officer. I will make sure he does not go out during recess again."

"I was hoping you would say that. If it happens again, I will have to charge you a very large fine," said the officer sternly.

"I understand. Thank you," said Lynne.

The policeman opened the truck and Crackers jumped out. He was so happy to get out of there. He ran by the policeman and by Lynne. He ran in the house and up the stairs. He ran into Graham and Lynne's bedroom and hid under the bed.

Soon, Lynne found him and scratched him behind the ears. "Okay, Crackers. I know how badly you feel, and I know this will never happen again. This will be our little secret," promised Lynne. Crackers wagged his tail.

Stephanie, Kendall, and Laura rushed home after school to see if Crackers was there. They were so happy to see that he was all right.

"It's okay, Crackers," said Kendall.

"We won't tell," said Stephanie.

"But, don't ever do anything like that again," said Laura.

Crackers didn't know exactly what they were saying, but he knew everything was back to normal. He was very glad to be out of "jail".

Chapter Seven

Crackers Saves Kendall

Crackers loved to play outside with Stephanie, Kendall, Laura, and the Brian Road kids. Brian Road was the name of the street where Crackers and his family lived. It was a dead-end street, and that made it very safe.

Saturday was Crackers' favorite day because the children didn't have to go to school. They would all gather at the bottom of Brian Road and wait for Graham. The kids would cheer and clap when Graham came out to play with them. Graham loved to play with the children so much that, sometimes, Lynne called him her fourth child. Since Graham's last name was Morgan, Brian Road was known as Mr. Morgan's playground.

One Saturday in May, everyone was playing a game called "Throw the Ball and Hide". Whoever was "it" threw the ball to the top of Brian Road. It was Crackers' job to run after the ball while the kids and Graham ran and hid. Crackers would catch the ball by picking it up in his mouth. He would then run back down Brian Road to tag one of the players. Of course, by the time Crackers came barreling down Brian Road, everyone was out of sight. This was Crackers' clue to look behind trees, in garages, behind bushes, behind houses; anywhere he could think of. Crackers always found someone, and when that happened, he would touch them with the ball. Then that person was "it", and that person would throw the ball, and the game started all over again.

Later that day, Graham went to town to do some errands. Some of the children went home while others continued to play. Laura went to Carrie's house, and Stephanie invited Diane to come to her house and play. Kendall and Michael decided to continue playing outside. Kendall and Michael were good friends and were always looking for new adventures. This particular day, the adventure was a little more than they bargained for.

Kendall and Michael decided to climb the tallest oak tree in the neighborhood. It happened to be in Michael's front yard, which was across the street from Kendall's house. No one had ever dared to climb it before, but Kendall and Michael were very brave and loved to try new things.

Kendall started up the tree first. "Come on, Michael," she said, "this is going to be so much fun."

"Okay," Michael yelled up to Kendall, and he began to climb the tree.

Kendall and Michael were very careful. They put one foot on one branch and pulled themselves up to the next branch. One branch after the other, Kendall and Michael climbed higher and higher. Soon they were up so high in the tree, they couldn't climb any higher. Kendall and Michael were at the top of the highest oak tree in the neighborhood. No one could see them. They had found the perfect hiding place. Kendall and Michael thought it was very "cool" and hid way up in the tree all afternoon.

Crackers had been roaming the neighborhood searching for Kendall. He always had to know that Stephanie, Kendall, and Laura were safe. He had seen Laura go to Carrie's house and knew she was safe. He actually followed Stephanie and Diane into the Morgan house and happily received a doggie biscuit from Lynne. Then, he went outside to look for Kendall. She was nowhere in sight

Back in the treetop, Kendall decided it was time to come down. She was getting hungry and wondered if it was time for dinner. "Hey, Mike," Kendall said. "I feel like climbing down now."

"Me too," agreed Michael as they both looked down to the branch below. "Yikes," yelled Michael. "Look how far down we have to go."

"Oh, oh," said Kendall, trying not to sound scared. "I don't think my foot can reach that branch. Let me give it a try."

"Don't even think about it," cried Michael. "This is way more dangerous than we thought. Climbing up was great, but now we can't get down. What are we going to do?"

Just then, Crackers came loping along and laid down under the tallest tree in the neighborhood. It was in Michael's yard. Crackers wondered if Kendall was playing in Michael's house. He thought he had chosen an excellent spot because he had a great view of his house as well. Maybe Kendall had come home while he was out looking for her. Then, Crackers started to sniff. There was something very familiar about the air around the tree. The scent seemed to travel up the trunk of the tree. Just as Crackers was looking way, way up the tree, Kendall and Michael were looking way, way down the tree.

"Oh, Crackers. Am I ever happy to see you," cried Kendall. "Crackers, help us," yelled Kendall.

Kendall and Michael thought Crackers looked like a little toy dog because he was so far away. They knew that Crackers was a smart dog, but they didn't know how Crackers could get them down from the treetop.

Crackers realized that Kendall and Michael were in trouble. He jumped on the tree and landed back on the ground. He tried that about ten times but soon, Crackers realized he could not climb the tree. It was one of those rare moments when Crackers wished he were a cat. He barked and he howled, and he howled and he barked, but no one heard him. He decided to run across the street to his house and get help.

Crackers barked and scratched at the door. Graham came to the door and said, "What's all the fuss, Crackers? Be careful or you'll ruin the door. Come on in."

But Crackers would not come in. He ran to the tree, and then he ran back to Graham.

"What is it, Crackers? Did you chase a cat up that tree?"

Crackers continued running back and forth between the house and the tree. Finally, Graham walked over to the tree and looked up into the tree expecting to see a cat. Imagine Graham's surprise when he saw Kendall and Michael way, way up in the tree.

"Oh, my goodness," cried Graham. "How on earth did you two climb way up there? Don't move," he warned Kendall and Michael. "I am going to have to call the fire department to rescue you two. They have tall ladders and they will be able to reach you and bring you down safely."

Kendall and Michael blinked at each other and tried not to cry. They were sorry to cause so much trouble.

Soon, all the neighbors and the Brian Road kids gathered around the tree and looked up at

Kendall and Michael. Everyone told them to stay calm, and everything would be all right.

The fire engine's siren could be heard in the distance. When the fire truck arrived, the firemen carried their long ladder to the tree. One fireman began climbing up the tree. The fireman carried Michael down first. Kendall said it was only fair for Michael to go first because climbing the tree had been her idea. Next, Kendall was safely carried down from the top of the tree. All the Brian Road kids cheered.

When Kendall reached the ground, she thanked the fireman and she thanked her father. Then, she threw her arms around Crackers and said, "I love you, Crackers. You're the best dog in the world."

Crackers jumped on Kendall and licked her face and wagged his tail happily. He just loved being a hero.

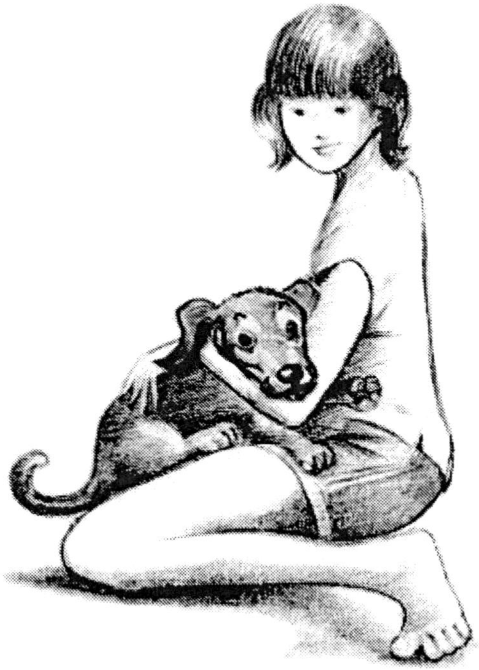

Chapter Eight

Laura Gives Crackers a Makeover

Hooray! It was April school vacation, and all the Brian Road kids were thrilled. Kendall and her friends went up to Mitch's house on Oakland Parkway and spent the first day of vacation swinging from his tree fort swing. It went up higher than his house. Mitch's mom would nervously watch the kids from her kitchen window as they swung by. She wondered if their parents knew just how high the swing was.

Stephanie visited her friend, Mary Ellen, who lived in the next block. Mary Ellen's parents both worked, so no one was home at Mary Ellen's house. Sometimes, Stephanie and Mary Ellen would be naughty. They would make random telephone calls to strangers and say silly things like; "Is your refrigerator running?" The person would say, "Yes." Then Stephanie or Mary Ellen would say, "Well, you better go catch it!" Then they would hang up. They thought it was hilarious and never told anyone what they were doing.

Laura stayed home and invited her friend, Jenny, over to play. Jenny had a parakeet whose name was Echo and a dog whose name was Mandy. She brought them with her. Laura also had a parakeet named Tweedle. Tweedle drove Crackers crazy. However, Crackers was a good dog and, therefore, put up with Tweedle.

Laura and Jenny read somewhere that birds liked classical music. They decided to take the birds out of their cages and let them fly around in Laura's bedroom while classical music was playing on a CD.

Crackers and Mandy were not allowed in the bedroom and had to stay outside the room.

Crackers felt very uncomfortable in this situation. He began to whine and paw at Laura's door.

Lynne was doing the laundry and could hear Crackers whining and scratching the door. "What is the matter, Crackers? What is going on inside that room?" asked Lynne.

Lynne opened the door to Laura's room just in time to see Tweedle and Echo fly across the room. They flew straight at her and then flew out of the bedroom. Laura and Jenny screamed. Mandy and Crackers barked, and they all ran after the birds. Lynne fell over the laundry basket, and clothes went everywhere.

Round and round everyone went. Dogs were barking, feathers were flying, little girls were screaming, and one mother was angry. Just then, Kendall walked in the front door, was totally amazed at the commotion, and – the birds flew out the door!

"Oh, no," screamed Laura. "Tweedle! Come back!"

"Who knew?" said Kendall.

But, it was too late. The birds flew up to the telephone wires and down the street.

Mrs. Robbins, a neighbor, was in her kitchen looking out the window. She could have sworn she saw two parakeets fly by. She immediately called her eye doctor to make an appointment.

Luckily, Jenny had forgotten to close the door of the screened-in porch of her house. Echo, followed by Tweedle, flew right into the porch and into Echo's cage. Jenny's mother was shocked to see Echo and Tweedle flying into the room, as you can imagine. She called Jenny to find out what was going on and to tell Jenny and Laura that their birds were safe.

Laura picked up Tweedle's cage and ran with Jenny, Crackers, and Mandy, to Jenny's house. They were very thankful that Echo and Tweedle were safe. Laura put Tweedle in his cage, picked it up, and with Crackers loping along beside her, went home.

Lynne put Tweedle in a quiet section of the house and covered his cage so he could rest after his harrowing experience. Lynne wished that Graham had been there to see the whole thing, but he was at work. She thought it would be a difficult thing to explain to him. You almost had to be there to experience the whole catastrophe. Lynne's nerves were frazzled. Laura knew she had better play quietly for the rest of the day.

As always, when Stephanie, Kendall, and Laura were upset, Crackers was there to cheer them up. He followed Laura to her room but couldn't go inside because the door was left only slightly ajar. He began to poke at the door with his nose. Laura was lying on her bed and laughed when she saw Crackers' nose in the doorway.

"Come here, Mr. Moo," said Laura. (No one could remember where that name came from or why it pertained to Crackers. It was just one of those things.) "Mr. Moo, we need to do something special to make up for all the fuss today."

Crackers pushed the door open with his nose and went right up to Laura. He put his two front paws on her bed, got his face as close to hers as possible and took a big lick.

"Yuck, Crackers. Your breath smells," said Laura disgustedly. "I think you need to improve yourself, and I think I am the one to help you. First, we will brush your teeth."

Laura didn't want to use her toothbrush on Crackers teeth, so she used Stephanie's. Crackers had to stand on his hind legs with his front paws on the sink. He felt ridiculous.

"Open wide, Crackers. That's good. Don't squirm. You need a makeover," insisted Laura.

After Laura cleaned Crackers' teeth, he caught a glimpse of himself in the mirror. He thought he must be ill because he was foaming at the mouth. Laura didn't seem to notice. Of course, she knew it was from the toothpaste.

Next, Laura filled the bathtub with water and put in Lynne's favorite bubble bath. Then she put

Crackers in the tub. This was not easy. Crackers was not very helpful, but Laura lifted his front paws onto the tub and then went around behind Crackers and picked up his back paws. Before he knew it, Crackers slipped, head first, into the tub.

Laura lathered Crackers with a bar of soap. His black fur was now almost all white. Next, Laura got the sand bucket she played with when they went to the Cape. She filled it with water and poured bucket after bucket over Crackers. He knew Laura was trying to help him, but he wondered if she was going just a little too far. Finally, his bath was over.

Crackers did not wait for Laura to help him out of the tub. He jumped up and out. If the bathroom door had been open, he would have run out. However, he was stuck inside the bathroom with Laura. He shook himself and shook himself to get dry, and water flew everywhere. Laura tried to protect herself with a towel, but not in time. Laura was almost as wet as Crackers. Water was dripping down the bathroom walls. Even the ceiling was dripping. It was not a pretty sight.

Next, Laura pulled out the hair dryer from the closet and began blow-drying Crackers' fur. Crackers hated the noise. The only thing that made it bearable was the fact that Laura was brushing his coat. Oh, that felt so good. Finally, Crackers was dry and clean. He looked good.

"You're not finished yet, Crackers," said Laura as she put on his collar and used it to pull him into her room. Laura shut the door keeping Crackers inside.

Crackers jumped onto Laura's bed and thought it was time to take a nap. Just as he was about to fall asleep, Laura came at him with a scissors in her hand. Crackers' instincts told him to run, but Laura was too close with that scissors.

"It's all right, Mr. Moo," said Laura sweetly. "Your whiskers are unbecoming. They are way too long. You need a trim."

Laura began snipping the whiskers around Crackers' nose. Then she trimmed his eyebrows. Crackers wondered if she was trying to make him into a seal!

Next, Laura opened one of her dresser drawers and removed a bandana and a pair of sunglasses. She promptly tied the bandana around Crackers' head and placed the sunglasses on his nose. Then Laura did the most shocking thing of all. She pulled out a tube of lipstick and drew lips around Crackers' mouth.

"Laura is not trying to make me into a seal," thought Crackers. "She is making me into a girl!"

Crackers bolted for the door, which at that exact moment was being opened by Lynne carrying her basket of laundry. Lynne was so shocked when she saw Crackers, she tripped over him. The basket of laundry fell, and clothes fell all over for the second time that day.

Meanwhile, Graham was just getting home from work and was walking in the door. "Hello, everybody. I'm home," said Graham, looking forward to a nice rest. "Where is everyone?"

Crackers flew by him in a flash and left Graham scratching his head and asking, "What was that?" Graham decided to follow Crackers.

Crackers continued running up the street. He wanted to shake off his sunglasses and bandana and push some grass around to get rid of the lipstick. But all of a sudden, he saw Stephanie and Mary Ellen crying in Mary Ellen's front yard. There was a man shaking his finger and yelling at them. Crackers didn't like that at all. He forgot about his ridiculous appearance and ran for the man.

The man was Mary Ellen's next-door neighbor. He saw something very strange headed straight toward him. He had no idea what it was, but he stopped yelling, and his jaw fell open. He turned and ran as fast as he could into his house and slammed the door. He made it just in time.

It happened that one of the girls' funny calls had been made to Mr. Blake, Mary Ellen's neighbor. He knew that the girls were being rude by making the calls, and he was upset. He had come over to tell them to stop until Crackers chased him inside.

"Crackers, is that you? You look weird," sniffed Stephanie as she patted her dog. Then Stephanie saw her father coming toward her, followed by her mother, Laura, and Kendall. Stephanie began to cry harder because she knew she would have to tell the truth about the phone calls.

Both Stephanie and Mary Ellen told the truth to Lynne and Graham. They promised never to misuse the phone again. Mary Ellen went to her house and Graham, Lynne, Stephanie, Kendall, Laura, and Crackers went home.

Laura had to clean the lipstick off Crackers, wash the bathtub, and pick up the laundry. Stephanie had to write a letter of apology to Mr. Blake. Kendall went out to play with the Brian Road kids and felt happy that, for once, she was not in trouble. Lynne told Graham about the whole day from the bird adventure to Crackers' makeover. Graham laughed and said that it was good to be home.

Later that afternoon, as the sun was fading, Crackers went to take a nap in one of his favorite outside places. Unfortunately, it was in the middle of Brian Road! The sun had warmed the road, and Crackers thought it was the perfect place to rest.

Luckily, the neighbors were all very understanding.

As the Brian Road parents came home from a hard day of work, they had to drive their cars around Crackers who was lying on the road. Sometimes, if they had a big car, they would have to get out of their car and move Crackers over a little so they could get by. He didn't mind being moved. Crackers was just thankful that Laura hadn't made him look like a cat.

Printed in the United Kingdom
by Lightning Source UK Ltd.
124265UK00002B/258/A